AS SHE WALKED

AS SHE WALKED

EVANGELINE CAIN

Rev. date: 04/18/2019

To order additional copies of this book, contact:
Xlibris
1-888-795-4274
www.Xlibris.com
Orders@Xlibris.com
759849

Contents

Introduction

In memory of . . .

As I walk, I slowly weave the thread of the presence of the goddess into my sacred life. Mama, as a daughter, I always felt denied of the essence of the trail of the goddess, and I come to see that I was always welcomed, and I was invited to embrace a beautiful sacred life. At one point, I truly believed more in self-doubt than in the love that was being offered to me.

Mama said, "Come, my love, you who is wild and free. I will stay close to you until you are strong enough to do it without me." I am the daughter who is afraid, the one who holds magic and power in her hands, the one who is fearful to fully embrace the path that scares her, afraid of the truth of her being, she who has walked wounded and thirsty. "I see you, my dear, even though you have been fearful of me."

Chapter 1

Message from Venus

Hi. I am Mother Venus, the goddess of the land. My domain is love, peace, and light, and if you are looking to rise above the ashes of ignorance or manifest new abundance into your life, I am your guide. I, my loves, have put in tireless efforts to pull you into my web of light which stems from my womb because I know you've heard the call within, you've even felt something tugging at your heart strings, and you've tried to distinguish what it is.

You know that from the well of our chalice, your womb knows who you really are. She knows your ancient feminine power that lives on. She awakes, my loves. She claims extended love and spreads it far and wide. She rises, walks in the close that resembles me with love encoded in her blood. She knows. She has a unique soul contract to fill and rise to the activation of her calling.

My dearest daughters and sons, I send you celestial blessings from afar. I am here today as a representation of the goddess because I have been told through the heavens that humanity is at a breaking point and people are finding it hard to bypass negative energies.

The forces of Venus are being opposed by negative energies that I will prevail and prove that I am more powerful than any opposing force.

She, the gatekeeper, only stands for love; therefore, all else is corrupt. She is the law of light, and no darkness can find its way inside the temple of my heart. She is a timeless muse who is never forgotten, rooted in love that goes back in time and protects us.

We say, "Oh, Venus, goddess of love, the woman to whom a thousand temples rise, the goddess gowned by silken wraps, her title known as lap of luxury, Venus, when the cave of darkness tries to pull us in, we shall build a starship to take us directly to you for you awaken heartfelt emotions, the woman who gifts us with spiritual nutrition. She, the womb who provides the land with milk and honey, I know that you are the guardian put on this sacred earth to create heaven on earth. You are the clay that molded to hold within you love, peace, humility, honor, and respect for all beings."

Venus, the goddess of love, has asked me to carry a message of truth to you today. Her first response was "Thank you, thank you, for not denying me my sons and daughters." She asked that you bring back the divine feminine in you, the feminine who has been lost and searching, trying to find her way home to self. She has asked that you unveil your mask and follow her instructions into an unfamiliar path, a path that is fruitful with promise, a path that holds the love that is encoded in your heart, and to rise, my dear one, to conquer all illusions and fear.

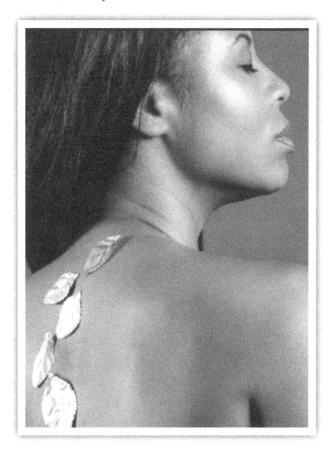

You are asked to look within and open the gardens of your heart and follow the authority that is being given to you because the world awaits to plant your seeds of intention, and so I ask you to defend your ancestors and carry their codes of love to dry earth.

I ask that you never deny me and to always defend my name for I am the mother of the earth who has protected you for thousands of years. I have left an image of me in you so you can walk in my image. As you come to recognize me, you will come to know inner peace and rest. As you walk dressed as me, you will discover that you are in the midst of experiencing a great transition into the fertile soil that incubates what is next to grow.

Inanna

Chapter 2

Goddess Inanna Speaks

Inanna is rising, my loves. She rises cloaked in the silk garnets of all of life's creation. She says, "Bow down to me for I am the gatekeeper of mysteries and wisdom untold. Do you hear me speak to you, dear ones? Should you dare look inside the secrets of the doors where I reside, then, and only then, will you see me waiting for you."

Do you feel my presence there, dear one?

My sister Sophia, the avatar, the cosmic queen, has arrived to hover over you and shelter you like a blanket, to carry you away from the ego and teach you spiritual alignment.

Come, my dears, I have been waiting for you, waiting for you to feel the warm that lives inside of me that has been sheltered from you.

Do you feel my love?

I am here.

Come! Come now into the temple, don't be afraid.

My dears, now is the time for me to pass my wisdom onto you.

Are you ready to feel enlightened? You must be ready for your whole existence will change as you will then, and only then, mirror the cosmic forces of the universe onto another.

When you enter this chamber, you will become one with the heavens. You will come to see what delight you can dwell in as you become one with me and Jesus Christ for I am my father's keeper. As you enter, there is no turning around, and nothing can hinder you from lifting the veil that was a mystery to you. All that you didn't understand will become clear as the veil is lifted from your eyes. When you arrive, peace on earth will become part of you, and love will then rise within your heart, and from that moment forward, you will understand love.

As you become one with the light of love, you shall receive love as you will receive in return the frequencies you give out. You shall free the once unbinding karmas of the world and start anew. You will be untangled from the web of bad vibes that once assumed you.

My dears, my eyes of love are fixed on you, and I see the real you through your pain. I see you through the joy you try to contain. I see everything, and it is my sacrifice to walk among you, not because I am high and mighty, but because I love you and I stand by humanity. I too, as a child of God, have free will and rights, and I chose to stand by you.

I asked for love and peace to assist God here on this journey to flow wild with the waters so I can create my fire that is of passion that burns for all of you. I, my loves, have felt the chapters of divine life unfolding before and lifted the veil to mysteries, and as each chapter unfolds, I have seen a new you being birthed.

I left a story for you, which is why my name is often talked about. My loves, I earned my respect, and I demand to be adored by you for I have sacrificed for thousands of years to nurture you and protect you.

I, Inanna, the mother of the earth, rise. I rise cloaked in the silk garnets of all of life's creation. She says, "Bow down to me for I am the gatekeeper of mysteries and wisdom untold...

Do you hear me speak to you dear ones?

Should you dare to look inside the secrets of heavens doors where I reside, than, and only then will you see me waiting for you.

My eyes of love are fixed on you, and I see the real you through your pain. I see you through the joy you try to contain. I see everything, and it is my sacrifice to walk among you, not because I am high and mighty, but because I love you, and I stand by humanity. I too, as a child of God, have free will and rights, and I chose to assist you.

I called upon the powers of my brothers and sisters to anoint me with love and peace to assist God here on this journey, to flow wild with the waters so I can create my fire that is of passion that burns for all of you. I, my loves, have felt the chapters of divine life rising before you, and as each page is turned, a new you is birthed.

I left a story for you. I earned my respect. I demand to be adored by you for I have sacrificed for thousands of years to years.

Chapter 3

Meeting Yemeya by the Shore

Oh, my little children, I am the grand entrance that demands respect for I am the mother who created you from my womb, an existence that only I can claim. Dear ones, the land would be bare without me, and there would not be you. And since we are here together, let's create heaven on earth.

I am Mother Yemaya, and I protect the land. I am the protector of the flowing waters, and I step forth when the dark vast openness of the water echoes your cries to me. I come to your aid when I hear fear in your voice, as I hear the cries of all my babies. This is when I appear. I show up under the crescent moon, grab you, and pull you in when it feels like you're sinking. I stand amid the waves. I am that portrait of safety, comfort, and grace. I am the mother who is standing at the ocean's tide, and I heal your soul with my water. Even if your eyes shall be closed, I will still unveil all mysteries that aren't understandable to you.

As I come to you in the language of the heavens, I reveal that there is a temple that awaits you, my loves, and as the doors swing open, you shall discover me standing there, standing for the true meaning of light and love.

You will be drawn to search the desert to follow the abyss, the map of divine love. Those who obey and bring the beauty of the heavens below to earth are those who are blessed. Those who walk with the great mother accept her oath and understand her sacrifice. They feel her pain because their souls intertwine Those souls, dear ones, know what it feels like to birth a new creation and can feel the pain as life bears down.

Those who deny the truth of their ancestors shall accept their own faith, as we all have free will, but they will spiral down with the dark until they accept the light. I walked, my loves, on the deep shallow waters, and it was not dry land. I scoured the core of the earth wearing the flesh of Jesus Christ. Yes, I felt fear as I walked with bare feet claiming that I have an open heart, a token of sacrifice, as a promise of protection, as an oath of love to come only than shall you open your eyes to see my offering. I kissed the earth, and as I walked, my arms were open, and I invited you in.

I am the lamp of one thousand blazing flames, the spiritual fire that is hard to contain. I am the light that finds peace in the dark. I am the midwife in which all life is created, and I am the nurturance to all that has ever been birthed. I am the reverence in which babies are placed upon the earth. Therefore, you can trust in me.

In case you forgot, I want to remind you that I am love. I am more than just a being.

I am more than just a memory that exists on the face of the earth. Although it may appear that I am not here with you, I am. It may feel as though I am just a legend smeared across the pages of faded scrolls, but my spirit still lives to always be revealed to you.

I am the expansion behind the materiality that acts as barrier of life. I am the garden that is recognized as the oasis of beauty. I am the wide-open perception that feels everything and pours it out to you. I embody the spirit of the earth through Jesus Christ.

This is why I ask you to enter the gates of love as it will strip away your old way of being. You will become enlightened and see that energy is everything and that so much love projects off me onto you.

All your burdens shall be washed away if you trust in my offering. I am the mysterious island, the monument placed upon the earth as a memory of me. Through this construct, I still see the world for all that it is, in all its beauty and all its cruelty, and I shall save you, my child, from the darkness that tries to swallow you.

After a life of storms and upheavals, you need someone to nourish you. You are ready to walk down the road of human history to discover your destiny. My daughters, I invite you to walk the sandy shores of your life to be able to witness the abundance of life that lives inside of you, to watch you clench your fist, raise your hands, stomp your feet, and throw away all that don't serve you.

I gently ask . . .

what is love to you, my dear?

To me, it is walking on a beach and experiencing that feeling that I belong there.

_____

_____

_____

_____

_____

_____

_____

_____

_____

_____

_____

_____

_____

_____

_____

_____

_____

_____

_____

_____

_____

_____

_____

_____

_____

_____

_____

_____

_____

Yes, I greet you. Imagine us doing the sacred fire dance of love as I transform you and perform the sacred union that transforms us into one.

Yes, my daughter, collect the seashells that are left behind from me as I clear the path. I walk beside you on that sandy shore within you, whispering my intentions for your life, mirroring a love you have never experienced on earth until you paralleled with the forces of divine love.

My darling, I ask that you allow your old way of living to diminish as you become one with me. I will use my ability of love to protect you and serve you. You, my daughter, must stand at the shores of your life, seeing it clear for what it is. Hold my image within your mind so that you never drift away from all that I offer you. You are free, my daughter, free to love me, free to love all things, and you are not contained by anything. My love is offered to those who dwell in the vastness of mysteries. I have always loved you, I am the mother you always wished for, I have been there this whole time, but you slammed the doors to my gates and looked the other way.

Photography: Jays Creative Photos

Why, my child, do you deny me? Why must I beg for you to see me for all that I am? Don't you want love that is pure, powerful, and innocent? When you turn your back on me, you shall hear me roar from the heavens, and I do this so you understand how I feel betrayed through my voice.

Chapter 4

A letter from Aphrodite

The Goddess walked through the dark night of her shadow, receiving downloads from her higher self. She was guided by the trees that nurtured her, the roots of the earth that filled her with energy and light and pushed her forward from the breeze of the wind. She found her way using the guide of the North Star.

Gaia:

Here we are, all the children that I love so much. The children who live inside of me. I came today, to clear all the black clouds that surround you, so that we can break the ancestral spell that was placed upon you many centuries ago, so that you may stand in the light with me. I came to bring justice to the children who look up to my example so that you may walk in peace and abandon negativity.

I place you on the mantle of the earth, here you will be able to shine bright and be seen for all that you are. You are, written in the stars my love, you shine so bright and as we turn the pages of your divine story we see that you are love. I sit with memories, of you when you were just a little seed. I knew how your story would be unfolding, a time when you were innocent and free. You loved without being afraid; you plunged ahead without being ashamed

All my wisdom is here for those who wish to study my offerings. I am Aphrodite the queen of heaven and off earth.

I am love

I am here for you

I've always been with you. I love you

I have never not loved you

My heart that is full of wisdom is being illuminated and brought to the front page to all those children who wish to learn my mysteries.

I am the middle ground between heaven and earth

I am the mediator that helps you understand the difference between love and ignorance. I am one with God as he is my creator.

I am on a mission for him not me.

I am here, to educate all those children who separate me from my dad.

I am the woman who comes cloaked in God's blood to reveal to truth about my existence that no one wanted you to know.

I am the light surrounding you. I am a woman of divine love

I am the rose that Jesus Christ brought to the edge of the shore, he created me from foam and attached a message coded inside of me to go and tell thousands what he did for me. I exzist, because of him.

I think it is time, time to open the vessel of your temple to allow love to come in.

To nudge yourself gently and say," my dear, it's time to enter the doors that await you... and diminish the darkness that surrounds your loving embrace. It's time to walk into the light of each day

In a place of stillness of grace.

To find this temple you must go on a journey into the underworld where you will be bare, stripped down from all the beliefs once believed, than and only then will you be ready to face all her fears. The underworld is a place where you can give love and attention to her imperfections and nurture any tender spots that come up and when you arrive you will be queen of earth Just like Aphrodite the Rose. Only people with pure intentions are invited thought these gates, so I ask are you ready? How can you become prepared to invite purity in.

_____

_____

_____

_____

_____

_____

_____

All my daughters who love me, listen to me now, do you hear me call out your name?

I ask that you remove your veils once and for all as its blinding your eyes. It is time for you to know the truth.

Come

Come to me my dear. I'm waiting for you.

Waiting to reveal all the mysteries of life to you. Don't be afraid for I am the light not the dark. I am love

I am the truth

I am here on earth to serve and protect you.

My loves, don't be afraid of me for I am Aphrodite the keeper of love and I have rose from the waves of foam just to show you love. I have arrived to show you the true light of the world. Jesus Christ himself gave me life. He created me and brought me to the edge of the shoreline and I became his servant here to create heaven on earth. I came to inform you through her example how to honour our bodies as women. She was sensual, but at peace within her own temple. She was adored for who she was.

She was the women who was once afraid to face herself, but then rises from the underworld naked ready to face her fears and returned as goddess of love and sensuality. She was the goddesses drenched in her own magnificence morning, noon, and night. She says," you earned the right to be comfortable in your own skin and you don't need to be shamed about a thing. Women weave the thread of beauty and make life much more pretty.

Know Is the time to rewrite the story of your life.

_____

_____

_____

_____

_____

_____

_____

I am your teacher, the mother who leads you to loving yourself. I bring healing to those who follow my instructions that lead into grace and confidence.

Mantra:

Everything I do today is a act of self- love. I love myself.

I am valuable to the world.

I accept myself when I'm vulnerable,

I "turn heads as I walk, because my radiance nurtures the land.

I "except myself just as I am."

Lord, I am grateful"

I was the goddess created from the waves of the foam and my inner beauty drove men crazy. I represent all things beautiful and sweet.

I understand as the great mother the feeling to not feel beautiful in our vulnerable states, but if you are reading this message know it is not a mistake and it was delivered directly to you from me.

My daughters, so you know who I am? I guess I should tell you my story! I am the rose that binds all of earth.

I am a symbol of love.

I was born from the foam of the sea and as the waves swayed and the pearls dropped at my feet I was named the queen of beauty and luxury. I, my daughters, floated my way to Greece where I was greeted with love. and given attire worthy of my beauty. My marriage to Hephaestus wasn't great I am a hopeless romantic and he wasn't. I loved, to bathe myself in the essence of the rose and I felt my most beautiful and feminine when I wore high heals, wore hot lipstick and sexy gowns to seduce him, but my husband didn't pay much attention to that and his lack of devotion towards me resulted in me having an affair with ares.

Many say, I was flirty, but I was not. To be honest, I was in love with a younger man who stole my heart. My love for him was so strong I became a moral to be with him. I shed, so many tears, because I was lonely. I prayed endlessly and one day God decided to answer me, so he formed a rose and placed it at my feet to remind me of how beautiful I am and to remind me of the beauty within the feminine spirit. Daddy wanted me to see, that I can hold myself together just as sturdy as a rose and this act reminded me of my strength.

Roses are known to bring forth the hiding of beauty and sensitivity. Roses are out angelic doorway that opens our heart to compassion. I step in to assist you so we can heal your wounds of our delicate souls. I want to help you align all your impurities, so you come to understand that women are vulnerable and it is ok. Roses, give up full permission to be that woman we once couldn't accept.

When I was exploring my essential innocence I found that roses stole my heart and brought me back home to myself. They touched me real deeply as they revealed to me who I really am. They revealed to me never be shamed of my sensitivity as it is all part of who I am. The rose is my eyes, my portal to a more gentler part of myself.

people often called me the sea goddess. Many women adored me, because I displayed love, peace and grace.

Speak to me!!

Ask me, To bless you with my grace and carry you until you have confidence, because I will of you ask.

My daughter, not everybody liked me, but I loved me so much and I got through my day using the same mantra I shared with you today. I am your role model for self- love. All misconceptions you believe must fade away as it is time to be gentle with yourself. You my daughter are a guiding light, your since of self - worth that brings her to love herself. I am your compass that enables you to feel confidence. This denotes the beauty a woman feels within- her guide to femininity. The sassy, silver, pink, red, and black parts of herself. When loving and accepting our feminine aspects that give ourselves permission to be vulnerable and soft, strong and brace. When we are accepting ourselves we become one with all facets of ourselves.

what parts of yourself are you having a hard time accepting?

_____

_____

_____

_____

What would need to take place so you could nurture the parts of yourself that you haven't been excepting?

_____

_____

_____

_____

Today we close our eyes and inhale and exhale the present moment into our lives we connect with the tides without saying a sound.

Stay ground my dear and feel everything that is coming up.

Take a moment to ask yourself, how it makes you feel as you step forth with nature and feel the breeze?

Do you feel safe?

Do you feel scared? Do you feel safe?

Do you feel free?

Whatever is coming up for you is ok, but it's worth acknowledging.

Let's say to ourselves; "Aphrodite, step forth and allows us to feel your love and grace as we need your support today. Bless my heart, so I grow with ease so anxiety moves away from me. Assist me, so I find balance, tolerance, and understand within myself.

Today, I hold a seashell close to my heart, under a crest moon.in memory of your good contribution to all the wise women who follow you. As we commend our fears upon you, we talk with our seashells close to our hearts as we journey, in memory of you as we visit the ocean." If we allow our soul to flow, in essence; to the river; we will live in harmony; we will find balance; and will receive love.

Day 1

Do you see me, my daughters, sitting on a cubic stone
between two pillars of strength and light?
My daughters, a goddess revealed herself to me, stood with so
much love. My dear, I saw you, I felt your blessings. She held out
her hand and asked me to soften into the expansion of my heart.
How can I resist? Her cloak unfolds into mysteries of sacred
love that weaves through my DNA. Yes, I'm living a full life.
Last night, as I explored my thoughts, I was still and silent and
discovered I was sitting with God and myself. I sat at the table with
the heavenly host. I come to see that none of us will ever get back
time that is lost. My loves, that time is gone. That time becomes a
distant memory that faded away in the sky. We can pick ourselves
back up, dust off, and keep following the light of God's love.
We can become elevated from all things and enlightened in the moment.
A clear mind guides us to our path using God as our compass. He
will lead us back to loving him and ourselves. I know this because he
led me there. Stay strong. Yes, sometimes we must endure the great
fight of life, and there will be many battles, but not all fights are
worth going to war, so stay focused, and trust that God is the way.

Love, Vange

Day 2

Mantra
I am ready for change.
I am willing to do whatever it takes to manifest love and abundance.
Daddy, I'm listening to your every demand.
Guide me. I give you my hand.
Let's just walk slow. I promise I won't let go.

1. The goddess wants to ask you, what matters the most to you in your life right now?

Day 3

"Sure I'm beautiful, but I am more than just that. I been through it all, yet I'm still standing tall. I am not living in a man's world. I am living in my own world as I pay my own bills and take care of myself. Yes, I am strong now, but I was once a broken little girl, but once I discovered not everyone had my back, I became my own best friend."

—Rika Demers

2. What way are you living that isn't in alignment to the vision you see for yourself?

Day 4

I need to unlock my inner wisdom so I can receive
answers to my issues that I can't solve myself.
I want to give birth to a better version of me.
God, please stand with me.
God, give me the strength I need to honor myself
and my true purpose peacefully.

3. Do you know your life's purpose my love? Writing it out helps you put it into perspective.

Day 5

People say I'm guarded, but I'm not, but I would like to change the way the world views a woman in her strength. We women are powerful beyond measure. Yes, I'm young but ambitious, and I believe I can have whatever I want.

—Rika Demers

4. Which 5 words describe the woman you are today?

Day 6

Sometimes the feminine forgets to lead her life from her womb, that place is stores all her energy, that place that connects her to her Shakti. Every now and then, she holds it all inside and resists letting go. She forgets to release, to let go, to be gentle with herself, and to move slow. Often she forgets that shiva energy exists. Just last week, she forgot again to unravel the tightness she held within.

But today she is allowing love in.

She allows herself to rest in the arms of her masculine because she almost forgot that feeling.

—Jorey Ann

5. What are the things that drain my energy?

Day 7

I love to see my students go out in the world and lead because I am a teacher and we all have our philosophies. I tell my students, "You can achieve anything."

—Kelly Barteaux

6. In all our lives we made choices that wasn't the best for us. When you think of those choices how do you feel and what did you learn from it?

Day 8

Mantra
Today I say goodbye to negativity and say hello to love.
Today I stopped being generous to those who do not earn my kind heart.
Today I no longer look for acceptance outside myself. I
no longer fight for anything fighting against me.
Today I choose to be happy. I choose to love me.

7. What are somethings that make you feel motivated in life?

Day 9

As we dive deep into the cave of our heart, our divine mother nudges us and says, "Don't give up." She asks us to give our past fears to her. She will hold on to them until we are ready to face them. She asks us to softly let go and don't allow worry and fear to take over our bodies. She is offering you love in exchange for your heart. You're safe as she would never leave you.

8. Are you holding onto something that left a wound in your heart? What would need to happen for you to let go?

Day 10

To all the little girls who are watching, never doubt your dreams, and when you do, simply look at me. I was given a chance, so I took it on myself.

Love, Jorey Ann

9. Write a letter to yourself giving you the close you need about a certain topic you couldn't get from someone else.

Day 11

She is grounded, my loves.
She has returned home to herself after a long journey of self-doubt.
The warrior she was but never wanted to be
is at peace within herself finally!
She opened her heart and found that her soul opened
to take her on a spiritual path into the light.
She now holds space in her heart.
She feels peace within.
She has finally healed her inner child.
She understands now that she was the goddess who was
trapped inside the illusion of her mind, but as she connects
to her DNA, she finds so much love within herself.

10. If there any fear holding me back from accomplishing my dream? Make a list of what those fears are and what life would look life if they where gone.

Day 12

"Life has knocked me down a thousand times, and every time, I got back up. It showed me things I wish I had never seen, and even when my eyes were closed, I had no choice but to see the lessons God had chosen for me."

The world revolves around
she who loves
Herself unconditionally
I trust the universe
To deliver to me what I need.
I know that God loves.
I trust the path before me
I can achieve my dreams
I am successful
I can find something to be proud of
In all endeavours I purse.
It is ok, to tell myself
That I am pretty.
I respond
To the inner wild in me
Beauty lives within
I trust my choices

Day 13

The Goddess acknowledges who you are. She knows you are a child of God, which is a beautiful mirror of divine love. The goddess has looked through your eyes at night while you were peaceful asleep and discovered that you are a celestial story of chaos and love. She knows you're most rooted when there is no clutter in the background and you are centered on yourself, that this is when you surrender and allow all your walls to come tumbling down.

She has discovered you feel most beautiful when you are attuned to your heart. She knows you feel most heartbroken when your reality is shattered. She knows pains set in when you are spreading yourself to thin. She knows you refuse to let intruders interrupt your peace of mind.

She asks you to relax and take a deep breath, my dear. I know your pain, beloveds, because we are all in this together. She is your divine mother who loved you from the very start.

She understands you because she too has been shamed out of her sensuality. She has been dishonored, not worth more than pain and scraps, and as a result, she felt undeserving for decades. Her strength has been waning, and her confidence has been decreasing. Momentarily, she was believing and clinging to the lies the world showed her, yet without her, the world just isn't a beautiful place.

She finally knows the truth about who she is. As she embraces a new metaphor, she feels herself transforming from darkness to light. It has taken many years to break the chains of conditioning she once believed. She understands that these theories she held on to aren't correct about who she is and that she is beginning all over again.

What beliefs have you been carrying with you that aren't true about yourself?

_____

_____

_____

_____

_____

_____

_____

_____

_____

_____

_____

_____

_____

_____

_____

_____

_____

_____

_____

_____

_____

_____

_____

_____

_____

Tell me five great things about you that you know are true.

1. _____
2. _____
3. _____
4. _____
5. _____

Day 14

Today we show up as a vessel in the image of the Goddess, she who holds all love and light inside. The mysteries of her love and her power have been sheltered from you.

What does love look like to you?

_____
_____
_____
_____
_____
_____
_____
_____
_____
_____
_____

What unique qualities do you possess that make you different from the rest?

1. _____
2. _____
3. _____
4. _____
5. _____

Day 15

Dear Goddess,

Help her awaken the goddess within, the madam who has slumbered, buried behind the ashes of all the sacrifices she did. We call upon the waters to come crashing down to cleanse the heart of any pain. We invite the wind, breathless as we still stand tall. Raise the winds. Bring it on. Washing was the wisdom of past pains so she can rise and come alive again. She is ready.

She heard the whisper within.

Day 16

The goddesses Gaia has always been known as the goddess who wraps us in her velvet cloak to shelter us, the mother of love who inhibited the earth and offered it her nourishment.

In a time before time, I heard a call from the cosmos that we, as women, hold so much beauty inside.

She succumbed. It was Gaia, the mother of the land.

She said, "It is time for us all to come together." She hated the air that which we are compelled to breathe as it felt like she was trapped in the clutches of pollution.

We must feed our thirsty souls the love it needs to grow beautifully. She said she implores of you and wants her memory to stay alive. "Water me," she says. "Love me and treat me graciously as I did for you for many centuries."

Day 17

Use your voice, my dear. Speak softly but loud and clear.

The goddess, she spoke. She spoke up when she saw abuse. She stood a little taller when powerful men tried to manipulate her into being what he believed she should be. In her moments of silence, she felt her feelings. She went deep within herself and felt what came up. Her voice was empowered by the goddess that swims within. She stopped, she took a deep breath, she listened, she felt, and then she stopped being pulled into illusionary realities around her and opened her heart to the truth of the matter.

What situation could use your voice?

_____

Why didn't you let your feelings be known?

_____

Does some part of you feel it's wrong to say no? If so, why?

_____

Day 18

Sister,
stand up, and be seen.
It is time to serve the world through your gifts.
Right now,
you are needed.
Free yourself from fear.
It is not your friend.
Let go
of whatever you're holding on to that
doesn't serve you.
Reveal the highest truth of your essence.
It's time, my love.

Day 19

Our divine mother is at peace within.
She, my loves, is grounded.

She built her life from the ashes dusted upon the earth, and when life came crashing down, she was afraid, but she also knew she could start all over again. She believed she could create something from nothing. She knows all too well what it feels like to claim and accept her feelings. She understands what love feels like. There was a time that she forgot who she was but was reminded that she is the momentum that flows like magic. She is the goddess in walking form who scours the earth devoted to the forest and love.

Day 20

You are deceiving yourself
every time
you believe that you aren't enough.
You are deceiving yourself
every time
you believe that you aren't pretty.
You are deceiving yourself
every time
you refuse to not see the truth.
Apologize
to yourself because you are worthy.
You are deceiving yourself
every time
you wait for validation from someone else.
You are the validation you need,
and validation comes from you.
Release the pain.
You're powerful.
You're magic.
You're beautiful.
You're radiant.
You're not broken.
You're courageous.

Day 21

Today we look at our lives from a place of pride no matter where we are.

If you have kids, it's crucial to understand that you are a great mom. Celebrate the great upbringing you did by putting up a picture on the fridge and share it with friends. You are amazing, my loves, and it's time you claim it. My loves, try to remember how good they are doing and that you are part of this. You had a lot of late nights, didn't you? So give yourself a pat on the back. You packed so many lunches. Doesn't that deserve acknowledgment? Think about all the homework you helped them with when you had so much in your own life going on. Remember all the times you had to be there when you hardly had energy for yourself? Honey, you are amazing.

Day 22

Place a picture of you and your children here.

Day 23

Today I walk where I am guided to go.
Will you follow?
Where will I be led, only God knows, but we shall walk slow
and gracefully into the unknown. We know that each breath
and each step leads to a trail designed for us to go.
Are you hesitant to go?
Yes, she walked, with her face turned to the sky, feet firmly planted
on the earth, entering many trails, some lit with love and others so
dark you'd think you were being dragged into the pits of hell, but she
kept on walking and connecting to her intuition through each breath.
She, my loves, has traveled through many corridors to
understand herself, discovering that she isn't powerless—
she is powerful, she isn't afraid, she is strong.

Day 24

What obstacles have you faced that made you strong?

_____
_____
_____
_____
_____
_____
_____
_____
_____
_____
_____
_____
_____
_____
_____
_____
_____
_____
_____
_____
_____
_____
_____
_____
_____
_____
_____

Day 25

It is time to heal our soul.
I know it's been one hell of a fight to heal your soul.
It's been a fight to love yourself endlessly.
It's been hard to fully embrace yourself.
It's been brutal trying to convince yourself that you
are loveable when you just don't feel it.
You moved forward and took a few steps back because
you didn't believe in your own capabilities.
Fear moved its way in, and just for a sec, you believed it.
You believed the story that you are messy, forgetting
that all God's children are uniquely designed.
Share your story.
Sister, speak!
Liberate the world.
Smear your story on the pages you see.
Check in with the girl whose story has been untold.
I bow and light a candle for you, my dear.

Day 26

Describe the fantastic woman that you are.

_____
_____
_____
_____
_____
_____
_____
_____
_____
_____
_____
_____
_____
_____
_____
_____
_____
_____
_____
_____
_____
_____
_____
_____
_____
_____
_____

Day 27

She is grounded, my loves.
She has returned home to herself after a long journey of self-doubt.
The warrior she was, but never wanted to be,
Is at peace within herself finally!!!
She opened her heart and found that her soul opened
to take her on a spiritual path into the light.
She know holds space in her heart.
She feels peace within.
She has finally healed her inner child.
She was the goddess who was trapped inside the illusion of her mind,
but as she connects to her DNA she finds so much love within herself.

Day 28

Affirmations

Life loves me.
I am in the process of positive change.
I allow life to give me what I need.
I am comfortable looking in the mirror, saying,
"I love you. I truly adore me."
It is safe for me to love myself.
I set myself free from pain and agony.
I rise above what others think of me.
I don't know what I'm doing, but God is my guide.
I trust the process that life throws my way.
The earth is my playground, so I'm going to start having fun in it.
I am a wellspring overflowing with love.
I am beautiful beyond measure.
I am love, and peace is part of who I am.
My happy thoughts create my reality.
I accept my body.

Day 29

Which area in your life could use a good cleanse?

_____

_____

_____

_____

_____

What must go today, my loves?

_____

_____

_____

_____

_____

How does it feel to let go of what made you feel unworthy?

_____

_____

_____

_____

_____

Day 30

Who am I?

_____

_____

_____

_____

_____

My bio

_____

_____

_____

_____

_____

My accomplishments

_____

_____

_____

_____

_____

CPSIA information can be obtained
at www.ICGtesting.com
Printed in the USA
BVHW031418230419
546275BV00002B/226/P

9 781796 028522